Ortho Easy-S

Patios

*Created and designed
by the editorial staff of
Ortho Books*

Contents

Easy steps to a new patio

Quick and relatively easy to build, a patio is an enjoyable addition to the living space—and value—of your home. If well planned and carefully constructed, it can transform your yard, setting off landscape features and providing a pleasant place to relax. Most patios are affordable. Materials need not be costly, and you can provide the labor yourself.

This book is for the homeowner who is fairly handy and willing to spend some time and effort on an outdoor upgrade. It provides simple, step-by-step instructions for installing patios, retaining walls, and walkways using a wide variety of materials. Whether you select concrete, brick, tile, flagstone, or concrete pavers, this book will help you make the right choice for your climate, site, and budget. And because no two yards are the same, some basic design tips help you develop a plan that suits your situation. You'll learn how to position high-traffic areas, reserve space for eating and entertaining, and build in vantage points and features that will make the most of your outdoor living space.

Once you've drawn up the plans and chosen the materials, *Patios* instructs you on the simplest, most straightforward methods of constructing patio surfaces. In almost every case, if you make a mistake you can back up and begin again. And you can choose the approach most suited to your schedule and budget. For example, you may prefer laying patio materials on compacted sand—a simple and flexible approach—rather than concrete. Both methods are included in this book, and both can result in a patio you'll be proud of. Within a few weekends, you should have a beautiful setting from which to plan your next outdoor project.

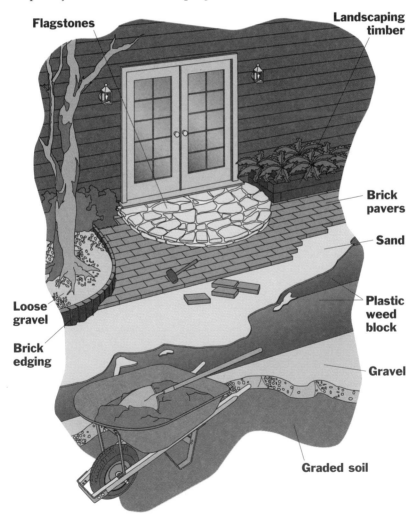

Flagstones

Landscaping timber

Brick pavers

Sand

Plastic weed block

Loose gravel

Brick edging

Gravel

Graded soil

Choosing Materials

Stone

The durability and natural beauty of stone make it an appealing choice for patios. Flagstone, available in a variety of colors and ranging from ½ to 2 inches thick, is easy to work with and beautifully contrasts with foliage. Fieldstone has a rugged charm and is comparatively inexpensive. Slate and granite have a classic dark look. Stone tile is precut into regular tilelike shapes. Although popular, stone does have disadvantages: It can be expensive, is sometimes slippery when wet, and has an uneven surface. And stone requires careful installation.

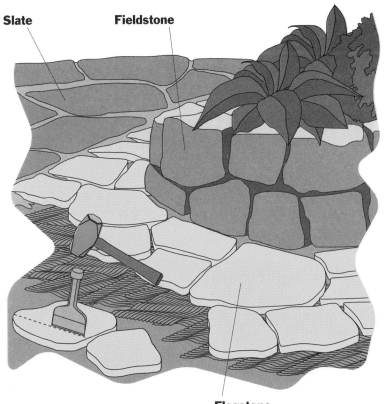

Slate

Fieldstone

Flagstone

Brick, pavers, and tile

Unlike natural stone, modular patio materials are uniform in size, so they fit together, requiring cutting only at edges and intersections. Brick comes in various colors and finishes, though glazed types are usually too slippery for patios. Brick can be laid in many patterns and blends in well with most settings. On the downside, brick is relatively costly, and in moist areas can attract mildew and algae. Interlocking concrete pavers are less expensive. They come in many shapes, are stronger than brick, and form a stable interlocking surface.

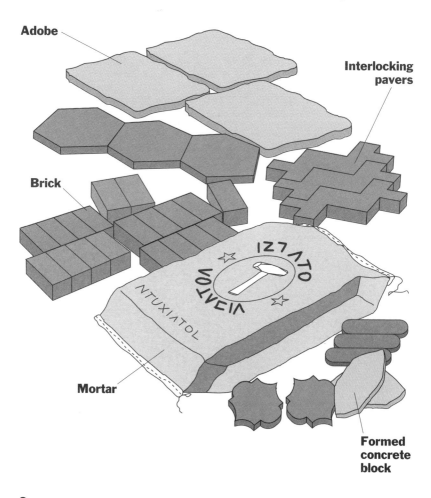

Adobe

Interlocking pavers

Brick

Mortar

Formed concrete block

Asphalt-stabilized adobe can withstand freezing weather. It comes in large tiles, so work progresses quickly. Adobe may be expensive outside the southwestern United States, however. Of all these materials, ceramic tile is the smoothest and easiest to clean. Tile comes in a variety of shapes, colors, and surfaces. Unglazed tile is less slippery when wet than glazed tile. Thinner tiles must be laid in wet mortar, preferably on a concrete base—a process best left to a professional. Tiles that are at least ¾ inch thick can be laid in sand.

Stone tiles (made of natural stone, but cut into standard shapes)

Grout

Tile

Turf block

Paver

TIP: If you live in a region where the ground freezes, make sure the patio materials will tolerate heaving ground, the stress of penetrating and freezing moisture, and the punishment of snow shoveling.

Loose materials

Loose materials work well for paths, nooks and crannies where there is little traffic, and as surfacing for accent areas. Loose materials are economical and very easy to install. Just excavate, lay down weed-blocking fabric, and spread the material evenly. Redwood chips and shredded bark are inexpensive but require refurbishing every few years. Gravel—including redrock and quartz pebbles—is available in many colors. It compacts well, but has sharp edges that can hurt bare feet. River rocks are smooth but tend to slide around and get slippery.

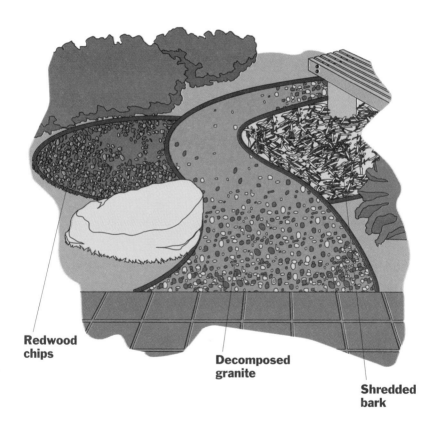

Redwood chips

Decomposed granite

Shredded bark

Decorative features

Added touches can go a long way toward making a patio pleasing and comfortable. Boulders or rocks can suggest a transition from the patio to other areas of the yard. Planters and garden benches bring foliage into the patio space. Edging materials can be mixed—timbers, brick, flagstone, upright posts— to provide visual contrast. Although they add interest to a patio, decorative features can be overdone. Choose a few and position them carefully rather than crowd several types together.

Designing the Patio

Map the space

On graph paper, draw a base plan (scaled at ¼ inch to the foot); include lot dimensions and all major features. Make photocopies, then sketch several bubble diagrams of locations and shapes for the patio. Consider sun/wind exposure, views, existing plants and trees (allow for growth), kitchen access, and foot traffic. Keep in mind that a path on which two people can walk side-by-side should be 3 to 5 feet wide; a service pathway (for one person) is 2 to 3 feet wide. For a comfortable dining area, add at least 32 inches to each side of the table.

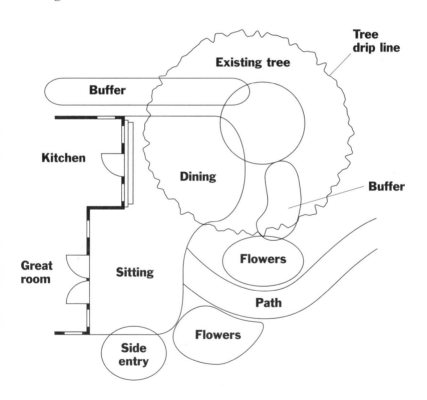

2 Plan grading and drainage

Drainage requirements depend upon expected rainfall and the patio materials. For example, a brick-in-sand surface will absorb some water whereas tile set in mortar will not. In general, a slope of at least 1 inch every 8 feet will keep puddles from forming. In bowl-shaped areas, you may need to install a catch basin or dry well. If you expect a lot of runoff, edge the patio with loose material, burying a drainage pipe if necessary. (See page 27 for these options.)

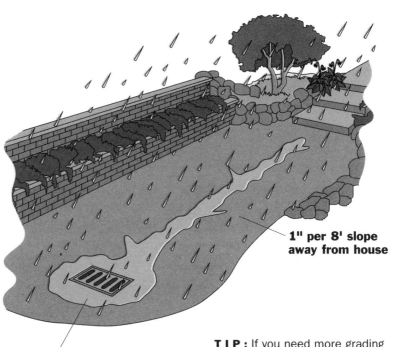

1" per 8' slope away from house

Catch basin for bowl-shaped patio

T I P : If you need more grading than you can handle with a shovel and wheelbarrow, or you require a retaining wall more than 3 feet high, or you want to retain a tree inside the patio, consult a landscape architect.

Pick paving pattern

Here are some popular patterns for brick or rectangular pavers. You can use more than one pattern on a patio, but be wary of the surface looking too busy. Simple patterns become monotonous on large patios; intricate patterns can look confusing in small areas. It may be worth the effort to sketch the layout, or to lay out the pattern on the driveway. Each design has advantages and disadvantages. Herringbone, for example, requires cutting a lot of small triangles. Jack-on-jack needs fewer cuts but quickly reveals unevenness or misalignment.

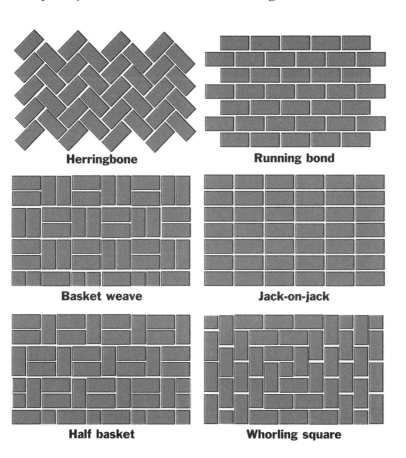

Herringbone   **Running bond**

Basket weave   **Jack-on-jack**

Half basket   **Whorling square**

Choose the features

Begin by highlighting planting areas, bushes, and trees that are already favorite parts of the yard. If you need a retaining wall, make a virtue out of necessity by making it a focal point. Perhaps the wall can also serve as a seating area. Space for planting can be created by omitting a section of patio, either as a dividing peninsula or along the house. Decorative pools can be surprisingly affordable. Consider stepping stones for areas that are not main walkways. Mix things up, but don't overdo it: Two or three features are usually enough.

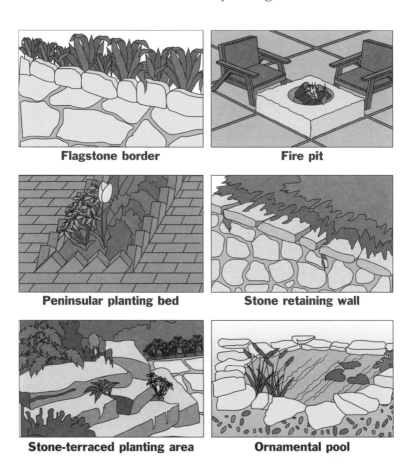

Flagstone border

Fire pit

Peninsular planting bed

Stone retaining wall

Stone-terraced planting area

Ornamental pool

Draw final plans

Draw a final site plan on tracing paper placed over the base plan. Double-check to make sure measurements are accurate. Use a garden hose to mark the outline of the future patio, and test to see that your furniture will fit, doors will open comfortably, and people will have enough room to walk. Check traffic patterns, such as from kitchen to grill area. Draw an aerial view, an elevation (a section of the patio from a ground-level perspective), and cross-sectional details of any structural requirements, such as a subsurface drainage system.

Get ready

To allow for waste, order 10 percent more paving material and weed-blocking fabric than the square footage of the patio. See page 34 for calculating how much sand or gravel to buy. Depending on the climate and soil conditions, plan on 4 to 6 inches of gravel and 1 to 1½ inches of sand. Here's a general materials checklist for most patios:

Bedding materials

- gravel
- sand for bedding (if not installing a concrete base)
- weed-blocking fabric (either plastic or fiber mesh)

Surface materials

- paving material to cover the main portion of patio
- edging materials
- fine sand for filling joints (varies according to how many joints and how wide they are)

Lumber for laying out the patio

- 2×4s for constructing batter boards and stakes
- 2×4s, 2×6s, or 2×8s for forms or guides along the edges
- strips of ⅜-inch plywood or redwood benderboard for curved edges
- 2×4s and ¾-inch plywood for screeds and screed guides
- plywood to kneel on when installing surface materials
- nails and screws

These basic tools will see you through most patio projects. Depending on the surface, you might also need a masonry blade for a circular saw, a wheelbarrow, and a drill with a screwdriver bit. A power compactor can be rented if you are working with a large area. You may also consider renting a small scoop loader for excavating. For tile work, you will need a tile cutter; for working with concrete, a bull float, darby, steel finishing trowel, wood float, and edger. If the surface you choose requires wet mortar, buy a pointed mason's trowel and a jointer.

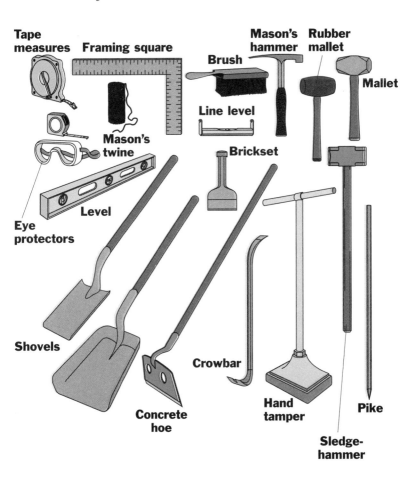

Preparing the Site

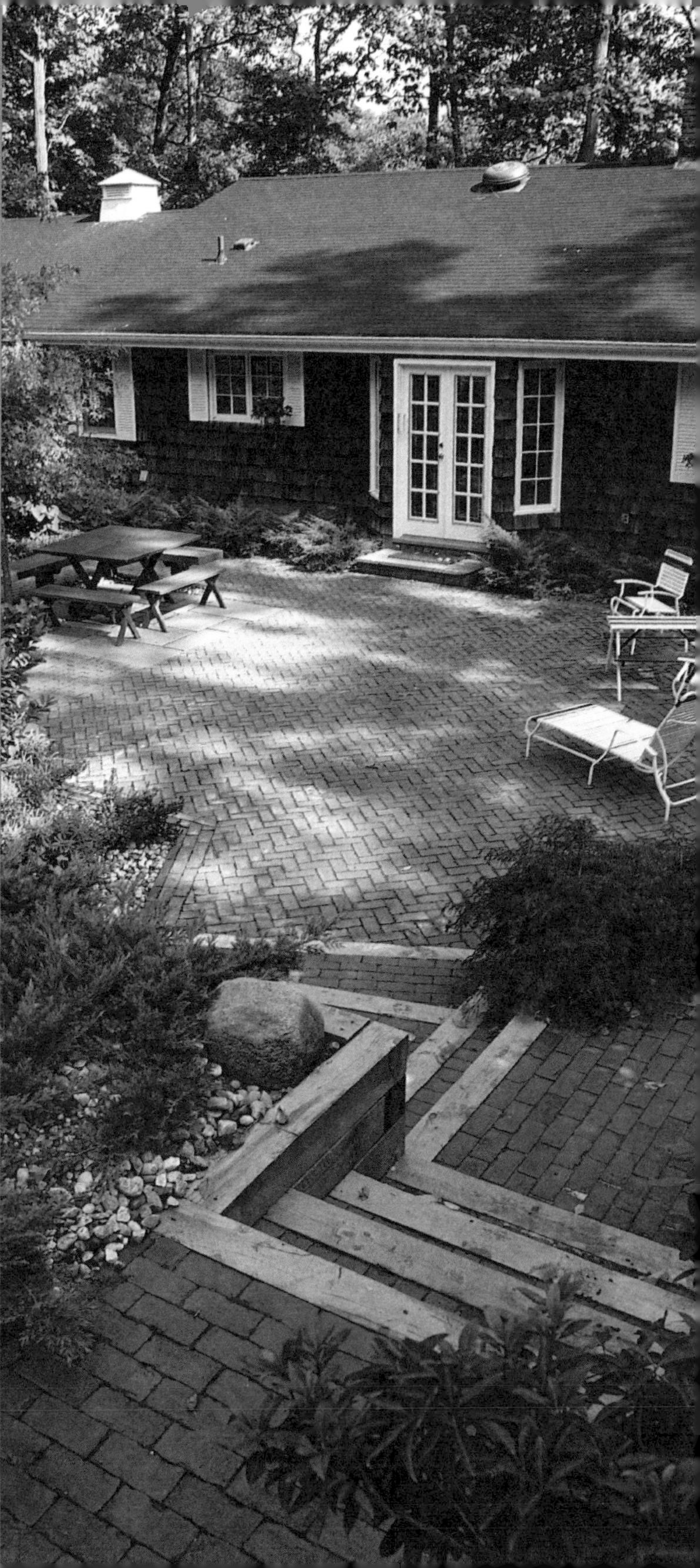

1 Demolish existing slab

Removing a concrete or asphalt slab requires no particular skills—just lots of hard work. In most cases, a sledgehammer and long crowbar are all you need to turn a driveway or sidewalk into a pile of rubble. If you have trouble getting it broken up, rent a 60-pound electric jackhammer. The biggest job is hauling away the debris. Unless you can use the rubble in your yard, rent a dumpster or debris box. Tell the refuse company in advance that you will be filling it with concrete—dumpsters have weight limits.

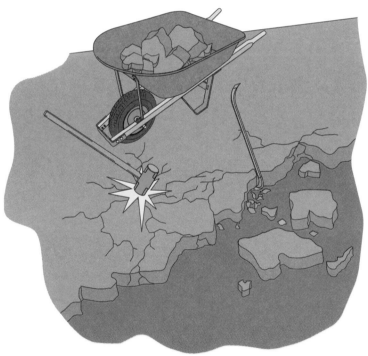

TIP: Always protect your eyes with safety goggles. Wear heavy-duty gloves, long pants, and a long-sleeved shirt. If you're using a jackhammer, use earplugs.

Rough-grade the site

In most cases, grading is simply a matter of leveling high spots, filling low spots, and making sure the site slopes in the right direction. You may have to rough-grade an area larger than the patio to make a smooth transition to the surrounding yard. If you remove plants, do not leave any roots in the ground that are thicker than 1 inch. Once roots decompose, they leave cavities in the ground that can cause the patio to slump.

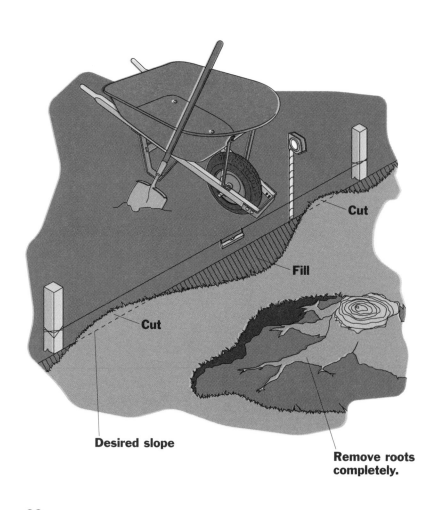

Cut

Fill

Cut

Desired slope

Remove roots completely.

3 Build batter boards

Make a pointed, 2-foot-long 2×4 stake for every 4 feet of perimeter. For each outside corner, build two batter boards. These will allow you to set up string lines that precisely indicate the height and perimeter of the patio. Pound the stakes so that they are 2 feet outside the patio, positioning them so the perimeter lines run between them. At the exact corner where the patio meets the house, drive a stake in the ground or tack a nail into the house for attaching a string line. (For laying out a site with curves, see page 33.)

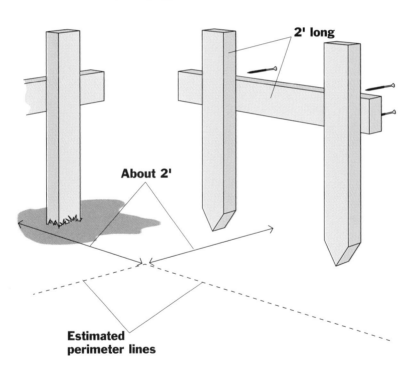

2' long

About 2'

Estimated
perimeter lines

String and square lines

String guidelines above the *sloping* patio sides. Mark a reference point on the house 6 inches above the final surface. Using a hydro level or line level, mark a batter-board stake level with that reference point. (If using a hydro level, check that both ends show the correct level. If using a line level, first center it on the string. Then reverse the level to check that it reads the same either way.) Set the slope 1 inch down for every 8 feet of length. Mark that point, screw in the crosspiece, and attach the string.

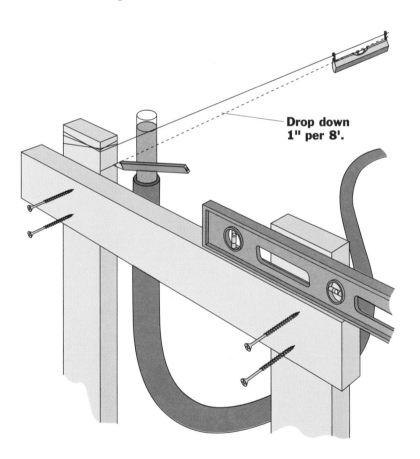

Drop down 1" per 8'.

Use the 3-4-5 method to check that the perimeter lines are square: Mark a point along the house 3 feet from the outside edge of the patio. Put a piece of tape on the string 4 feet out from the house. Measure between the two marks. The corner is square when the distance is exactly 5 feet. (For greater accuracy, use multiples of 3-4-5: 6-8-10 or 9-12-15.) As a final test, measure between opposite corners; the diagonals should be exactly the same. Double-check that the side along the house is level, using a hydro level or line level.

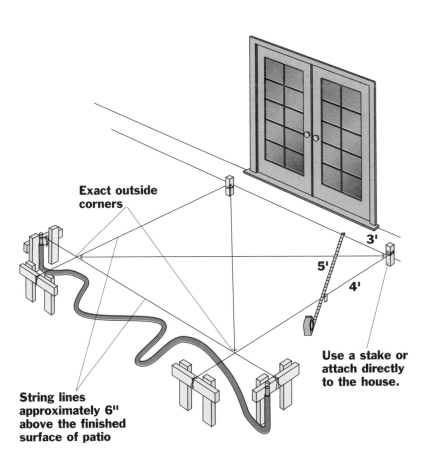

Exact outside corners

3'

5'

4'

Use a stake or attach directly to the house.

String lines approximately 6" above the finished surface of patio

Excavate the site

Figure the total thickness of the patio. (For example, 6 inches of gravel, 1 inch of sand, and bricks that are 2¼ inches thick require an excavation depth of 9¼ inches.) Remember that you positioned the strings 6 inches above the finished surface. (In the example shown, you would excavate 15¼ inches below the string lines.) Roughly dig out most of the dirt and cart it away in a wheelbarrow. Drive stakes and tie string lines in a 5-foot grid as a guide for final excavating. Scoop out the bottom to make an even surface. Cut the edges square.

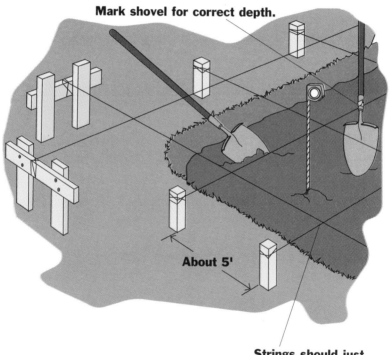

Mark shovel for correct depth.

About 5'

Strings should just touch perimeter strings without moving them.

Provide drainage

Because patios collect a surprising amount of water, it's important to build in adequate drainage. The simplest solution is gravel along the low end of the patio. If you install perforated drainage pipe, the system should end at a lower point on the lot or in a dry well. Build a dry well by digging a hole—2 to 4 feet in diameter and at least 3 feet deep—and filling it with gravel. For surges of water, install a catch basin, sloping the pipe at least ¼ inch per foot. It should drain into a dry well or some other catchment.

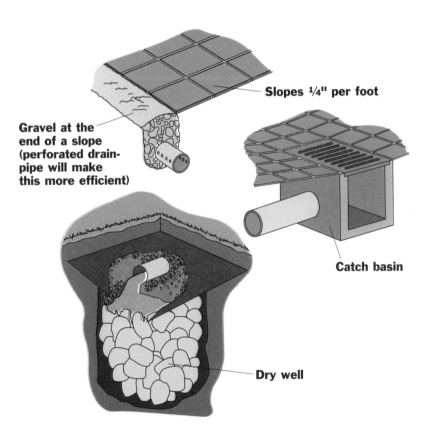

Slopes ¼" per foot

Gravel at the end of a slope (perforated drain-pipe will make this more efficient)

Catch basin

Dry well

Prepare for edging

Different edging materials require trenches of different depths. For example, with timber edging you may have to dig a trench deeper than the surface material. For brick edging, you may need to make the perimeter shallower than the rest of the bed. Some edgings, such as upright posts, should be seated in concrete. Consider all the elements of the patio and make sure you install them in the proper sequence. Cut the perimeter in a straight line, digging straight down and making sharp corners with a square-sided shovel.

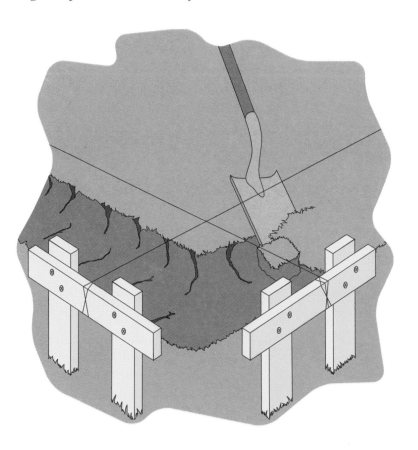

Edge with lumber . . .

Use 2×6 lumber or larger—4×4s or 4×6s have
a more substantial look. Choose pressure-treated
lumber or heartwood of cedar or redwood (not
"construction common," which will rot quickly).
Cut the boards to length, then set them in place using the
string lines as a guide. Join corners together with hot-dipped
galvanized (HDG) decking screws. Pound a stake every 3
feet for 2-by lumber, every 6 feet for 4-by. Double the stakes
wherever two pieces of edging butt together. Backfill with
soil, but not so tightly that it forces the boards inward.

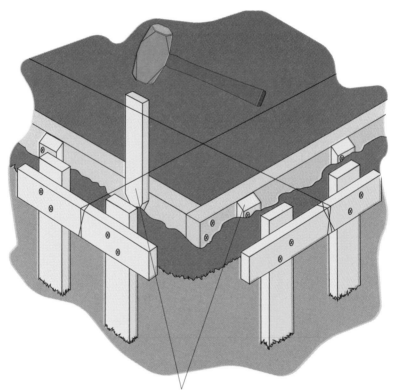

**Stakes made of 1×3, 12" long,
with the tops mitered after stakes
are pounded into the ground.**

. . . or use timbers

Landscaping timbers are treated to resist rot. Cut them to length and use the string lines to set them at the right height. Make sure they sit securely on a level bed of gravel. You may have to remove them and adjust the bedding several times. Drill through the timbers every 3 feet or so with a ⅝-inch bit. (Buy an extralong bit or attach a drill-bit extension.) Pound 2-foot lengths of ½-inch precut rebar through the holes and into the ground.

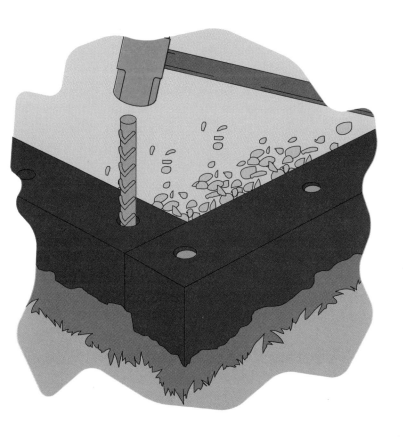

. . . or line up "soldiers"

Bricks on end, called soldiers, are sometimes laid on top of a concrete footing, but brick-in-soil edgings work well, too, so long as the soil is solid. Excavate and tamp the soil firmly. The tops of the soldiers will be flush with the finished patio surface. Take care to keep the soldiers straight. Use straightedges—very straight pieces of lumber about 8 feet long—as guides both for the back and the top of the bricks.

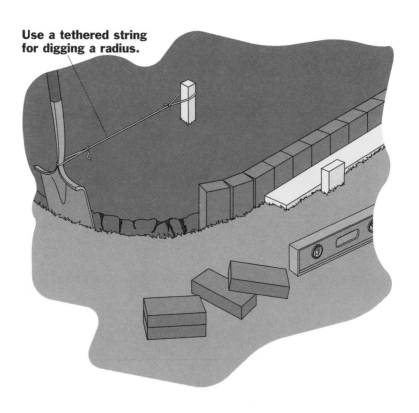

Use a tethered string for digging a radius.

. . . or edge with curves

To mark for a free-form curved edge, lay a garden hose in the exact shape of the proposed patio and pour flour along the length of it. Remove the hose, and you have a clearly defined outline.

Install redwood benderboard flush with the finished patio surface. Soak it in water first, then secure it with stakes on both sides. For a more substantial edge, double or triple the boards, then nail them together. Plastic edging material is best used for support only, so set it below the patio surface and cover it with soil.

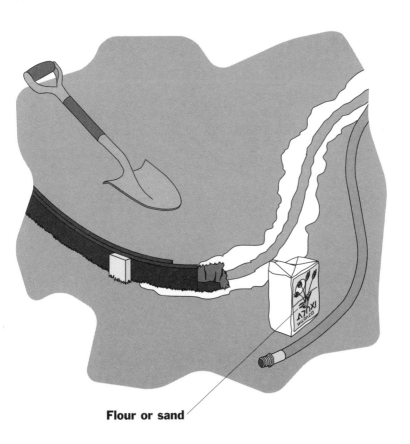

Flour or sand

Lay the bedding

Calculate how many cubic yards of sand and gravel you will need. Take the square footage of the excavated area, multiply by the depth in fractions of a foot, and divide by 27. For example, for a 6-inch-deep bed of gravel for a patio that is 300 square feet, use the following formula: *300 × .5 = 150.* Divide to get the number of cubic yards you'll need to order: *150 ÷ 27 = 5.56.* To be safe, give the supplier the dimensions and ask for an estimate. Order 10 percent extra for waste.

Estimating Sand or Gravel

Material	Square feet	Thickness		How much to order (includes 5–10% extra)
Sand	100	1"	.08'	.33 yard
	100	1½"	.13'	.5 yard
	100	2"	.17'	.67 yard
	500	1"	.08'	1.67 yards
	500	1½"	.13'	2.67 yards
Gravel	100	4"	.33'	1.33 yards
	100	6"	.5'	2.0 yards
	100	8"	.67'	2.67 yards
	500	4"	.33'	6.67 yards
	500	6"	.5'	10.0 yards
	500	8"	.67'	13.5 yards

Check the excavation depth to make sure it is fairly uniform. Fill low spots with gravel or soil and tamp firmly. It is critical that soil, gravel, and sand be well compacted, or the patio may develop "waves" after a few years. Use a hand tamper or rent a power compactor. If there is truck access to the patio site, plan ahead so the sand and gravel can be dumped in several piles to lessen the amount of shoveling you will have to do.

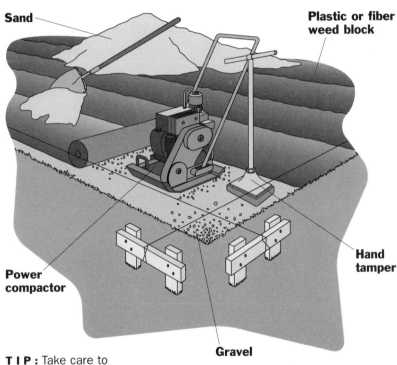

Sand

Plastic or fiber weed block

Hand tamper

Power compactor

Gravel

T I P : Take care to avoid back injury. As with any heavy lifting, lift at the knees, not with your back.

Installing a Patio on a Sand Bed

1 Set screed guides

In order to smooth the sand by pulling a screed across its surface, lay down temporary screed guides every 3 feet or so. Set 2×4s into the sand, or temporarily stake them if necessary. They should be seated solidly enough that they will stay at the correct height even if you stand on them.

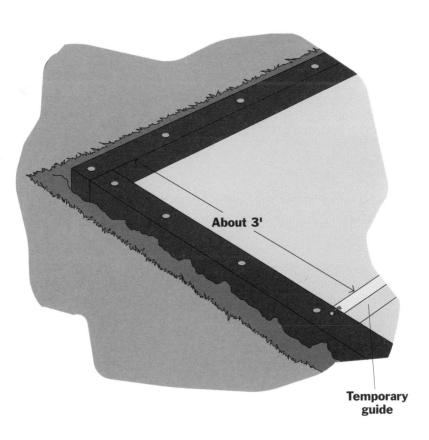

About 3'

Temporary
guide

2 Screed the sand

If the sand is dry, spray it lightly with a garden hose. Build a screed with a 2×4 and a piece of plywood. Attach the plywood so the finished surface will be ¼ to ½ inch higher than the finished surface to allow for compaction. Pull the screed toward you, using a sawing motion. Compact the sand with a hand tamper or power compactor. Add sand to any low spots. Remember that this surface determines how smooth the finished patio surface will be. Do not walk on the sand before installing the paving material.

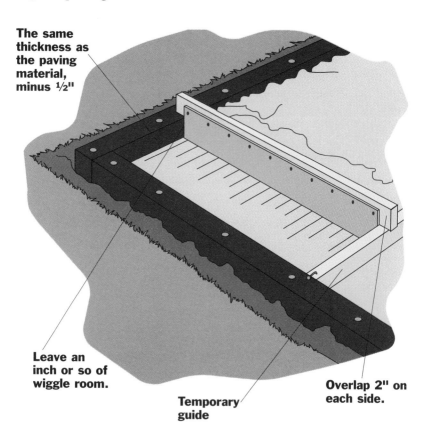

The same thickness as the paving material, minus ½"

Leave an inch or so of wiggle room.

Temporary guide

Overlap 2" on each side.

3

Crown a walk

If building a walk, prepare a sand bed that is crowned in the center so water will run off easily. Foot traffic will eventually pack down the center of a walkway more than the edges, so make the crown just a bit higher than necessary. To crown a sand bed, use a screed with a piece of plywood cut out like the crown, approximately ¼ inch higher at the center than the edges for each foot of width (a 4-foot-wide walk would be 1 inch higher in the center).

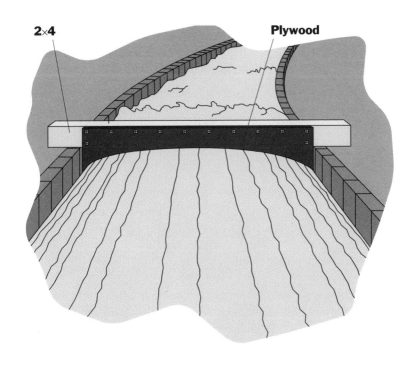

2×4

Plywood

Install brick or pavers

Set a row of four bricks in place along the guide board at one side of the patio. Repeat the process on the opposite side. Stake a guideline even with the ends of both rows. Install the bricks or pavers in 4-foot-square sections, setting them straight down on the sand, not end first. Check that joints line up at the guideline. To seat the bricks, tap lightly on a piece of 2×6 with a mallet. When a 4-foot-square section is complete, use a level to check that it is even. Use a scrap of plywood as a working platform.

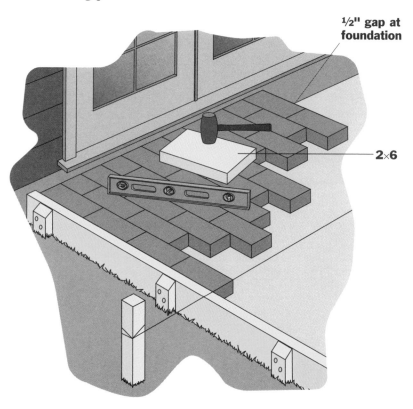

½" gap at foundation

2×6

To cut a brick or paver, use a broad-bladed cold chisel to score a line on all four sides. Then position the brickset on the score and rap sharply with a mallet. It should split neatly. A circular saw with a masonry blade is another alternative. Any roughness on the cut can be trimmed with a brickset or pointed trowel. When all bricks are laid, spread fine sand over the surface and sweep it into the joints. Lightly spray the patio with water, let it dry, then sweep in more sand and wet again.

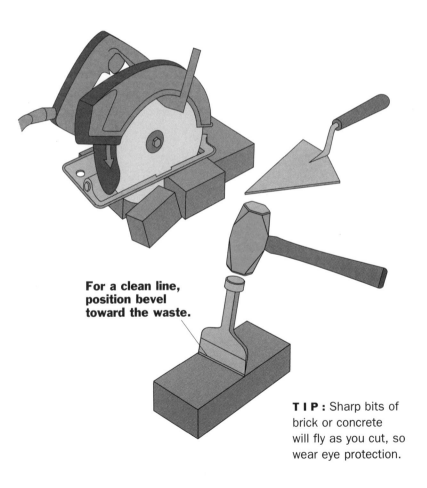

For a clean line, position bevel toward the waste.

T I P : Sharp bits of brick or concrete will fly as you cut, so wear eye protection.

Install flagstone

Flagstone can be installed directly on firm, graded soil that is well drained, free of roots, and covered with a weed-blocking fabric. A sand bed is easier to work with, however, because it can conform to the uneven surface of flagstone. Use the same procedure as for brick (page 40). When a stone sits too high or too low, pry it up and adjust the sand with your hand or a garden trowel. Combine stones of various sizes. It's best to lay them out in advance, arranging them into a pleasing configuration and making cuts as necessary.

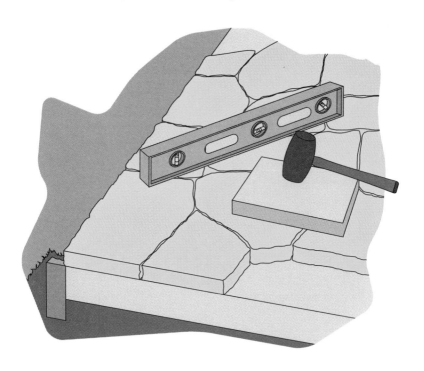

To mark a flagstone for cutting, place it under the adjacent stone and trace the outline with a pencil. Score the line with a chisel, prop up the stone, and split it with a brickset. Protect your eyes from flying chips. When all the stones are laid, cover them with fine sand and sweep it into the cracks, moving the broom in different directions as you do so. Wet the surface with a light spray, let it dry, then sweep in more sand and spray again.

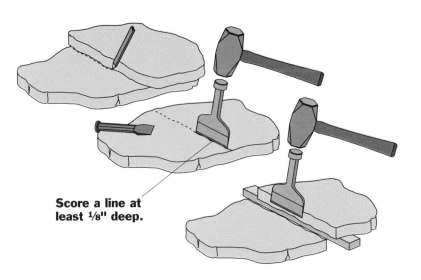

Score a line at least ⅛" deep.

Building a Concrete Patio

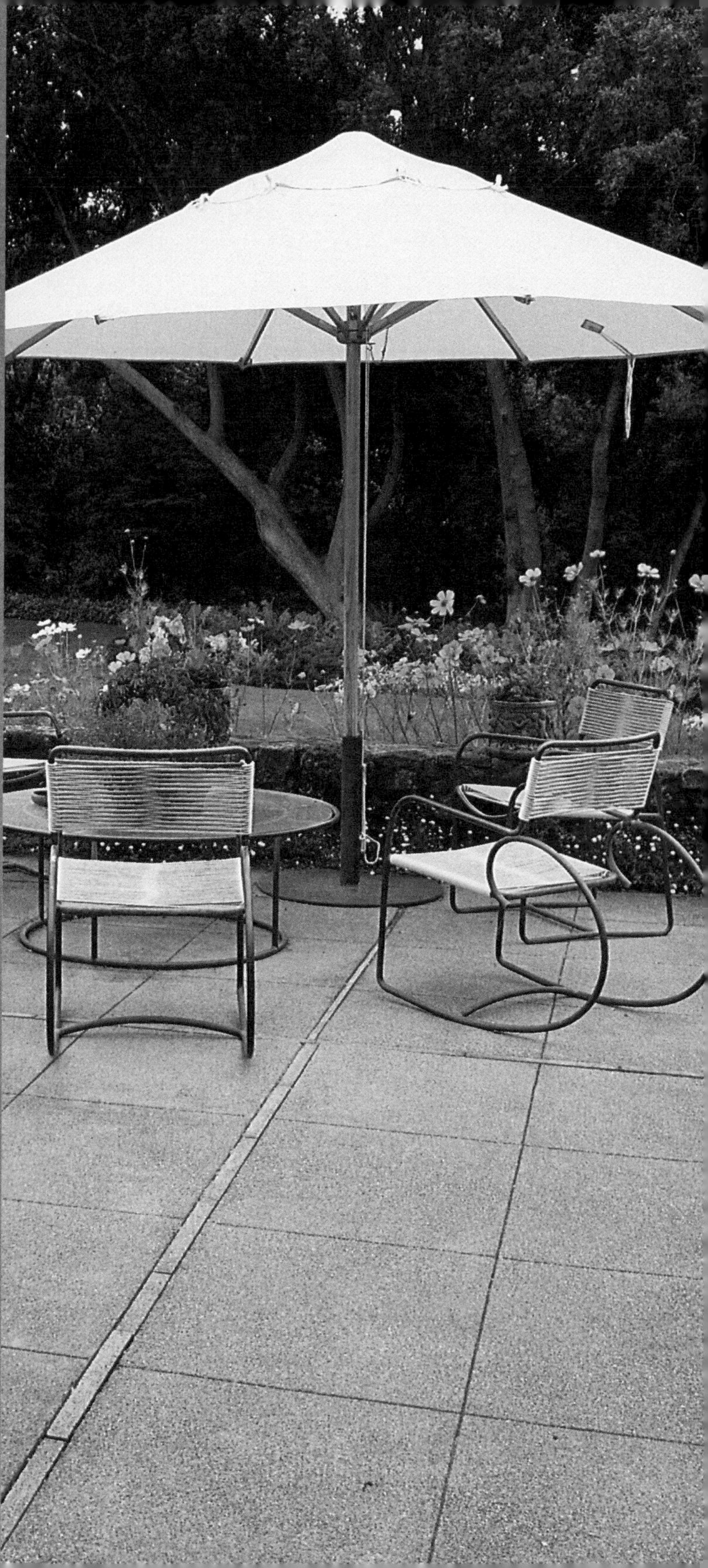

1 Prepare the ground

In most areas, 4 inches of gravel plus 4 inches of concrete will make a slab strong enough for a patio. (Check local codes; some may require a deeper footing around the perimeter.) Excavate the area as described on pages 22 through 26. Allow an extra 3 inches on each side for the forms. Because rainwater will cause runoff, plan for drainage (see pages 14 and 27). Remove all roots more than 1 inch thick, firmly tamp the soil and gravel, and add a weed barrier of plastic sheeting or weed-blocking fabric.

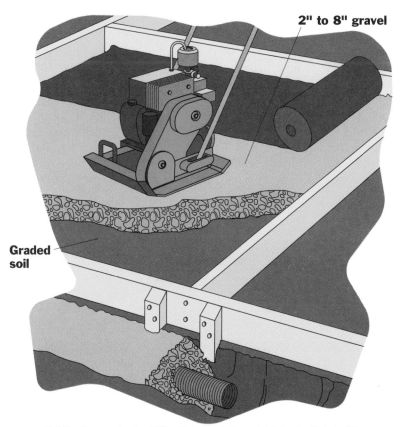

2" to 8" gravel

Graded soil

T I P : Concrete is difficult to install and tricky to finish. Use permanent dividers to keep the surfaces a workable size. If ready-mixed concrete is being delivered, have plenty of help on hand.

Get ready

Mix your own concrete only if you are working with small areas and prefer to spread out the work over a long period of time. In most cases, a concrete supplier will deliver concrete for little more than it would cost you to mix it yourself. Figure how many square yards of concrete you will need (see page 34). When ordering, specify ¾-inch aggregate (unless you're using a pumping service that requires a smaller size). Where winters are severe, specify that the concrete be air-entrained. Here are the tools you will need:

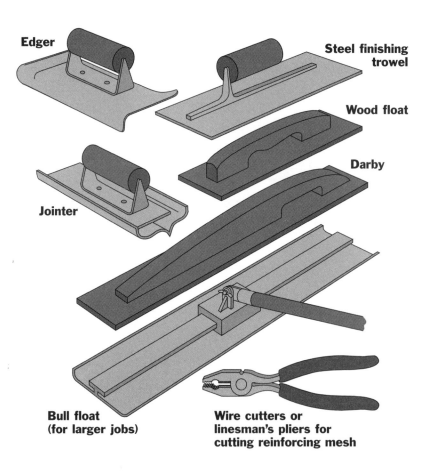

Edger

Steel finishing trowel

Wood float

Darby

Jointer

Bull float (for larger jobs)

Wire cutters or linesman's pliers for cutting reinforcing mesh

Build the forms

Use pressure-treated 2×4 lumber or the heart-wood of redwood or cedar for permanent forms and dividers. Anything else will rot quickly.

Wet concrete puts a lot of pressure on forms, so reinforce them accordingly. Use 2-foot-long stakes to back the form boards every 3 to 4 feet. Drive extra stakes at corners and joints. To ensure that the forms and dividers will adhere to the concrete, drive 16-penny (16d) HDG nails into the boards every 16 inches or so. Protect the tops of the 2×4s with masking tape to prevent denting or staining.

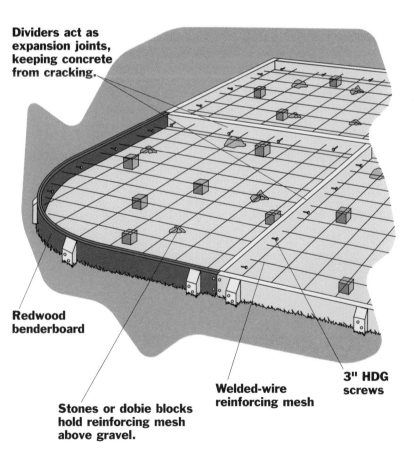

Dividers act as expansion joints, keeping concrete from cracking.

Redwood benderboard

Stones or dobie blocks hold reinforcing mesh above gravel.

Welded-wire reinforcing mesh

3" HDG screws

Place the concrete

Clear a pathway for the concrete truck to back up to the site. If this is not possible, use wheelbarrows or arrange for a concrete pumping service. Start with sections in the middle and work toward the periphery. As concrete is placed, use a rake to pull up the welded-wire reinforcing mesh so it is centered in the concrete. Use a hoe first, then a shovel, to spread the concrete. Poke the shovel into the concrete along the forms to eliminate air pockets. Hammer the outside of the forms and jab a rod up and down to consolidate the concrete.

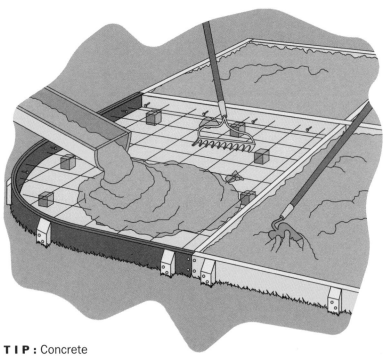

T I P : Concrete may cause skin irritation—wear gloves, long sleeves, and eye protection.

Use a straight 2×4 to screed the concrete (a slightly bowed one will result in puddles on the patio). With a helper on the other end, slide the screed side to side in a sawing motion as you move it forward. (Screeding not only removes excess concrete, but also pushes the aggregate below the surface.) Fill in any low spots with a shovel and then screed again. Do this quickly so you will have time to smooth the concrete before it sets.

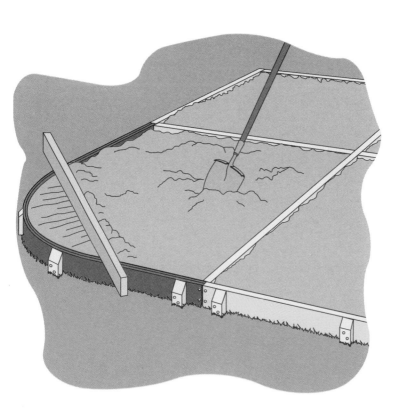

Smooth the surface . . .

Level the surface with a darby or (for larger sections) a bull float. Use overlapping circular strokes with the darby; push and pull the bull float, then pick it up and float a parallel, overlapping section. For both tools, keep the leading edge slightly raised to prevent gouging the concrete. To finish edges, run a pointed trowel along the forms. Next move an edger back and forth to make a rounded edge. After the concrete has set slightly, use a wood float for final floating. Work in light, circular movements. Three passes produce a slightly rough texture ideal for patios.

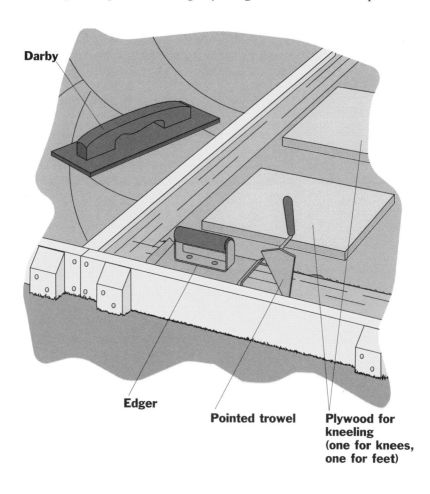

Darby

Edger

Pointed trowel

Plywood for kneeling (one for knees, one for feet)

6

. . . or expose the aggregate

One way to expose aggregate is to order concrete with rounded pebbles. After floating and edging, use a handheld sprayer to wet the surface with a concrete retarder. Cover the surface with plastic for an hour, then spray with a pressure washer. Another option is to trowel and edge the patio about ½ inch below the forms, then sprinkle the entire surface with aggregate. Use a darby to push the aggregate just below the surface. Refloat, then wet the surface with a fine spray. Finish by gently brushing the surface until the pebbles show.

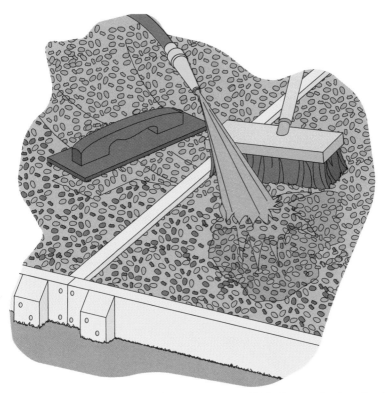

TIP : Minimize cracks by allowing the concrete to cure properly. For at least three days, keep it wet by gently spraying it or covering it with plastic sheeting.

7

Bricks or stone set in mortar

Make the slab below the top of the edging or form by the thickness of the surface material plus ½ inch. Dampen the concrete and screed a ½-inch-thick layer of mortar. (Limit the section to about 3 square feet—the area you'll cover in an hour.) Use dry ready-mixed mortar, or make your own by mixing 1 part cement with 4 parts wet sand. Set bricks using mason's twine as a guideline, leaving ½-inch joints between them. Seat each brick with a tap of a rubber mallet. Check for level as you work.

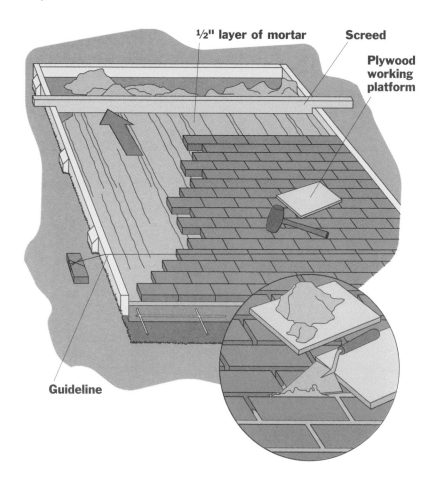

½" layer of mortar **Screed**

Plywood working platform

Guideline

Set stones in mortar, arranging them as explained on page 42. Wait 24 hours before finishing the joints. To mortar the joints, add ½ part hydrated lime to the mortar mix to improve workability. Pack it into the joints with a mason's trowel, keeping the mortar off the material as much as possible. Immediately clean up any spills and let the joints harden for about 30 minutes. Finish the joints by lightly tooling them with a jointer. Cover the area with plastic sheeting for 24 hours. Stay off the surface for an additional three days.

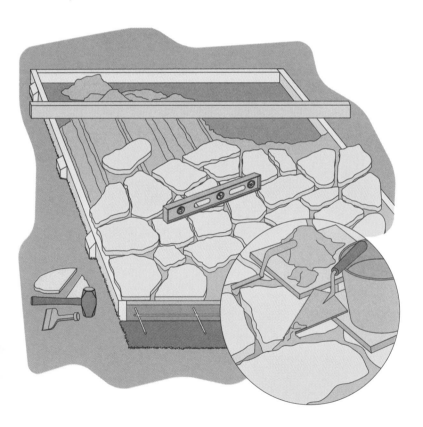

Plan the wall

Garden walls are useful for defining spaces, providing planting beds, and stabilizing slopes to create terraces. Elaborate walls and any wall more than 3 feet tall should be designed and built by a professional. For certain walls, you may need a permit. Suitable do-it-yourself materials include lumber, landscaping timbers, stone, and formed-concrete blocks. Garden walls can be beautiful as well as functional. By providing a contrasting backdrop and by raising plants closer to eye level, walls can create a striking effect.

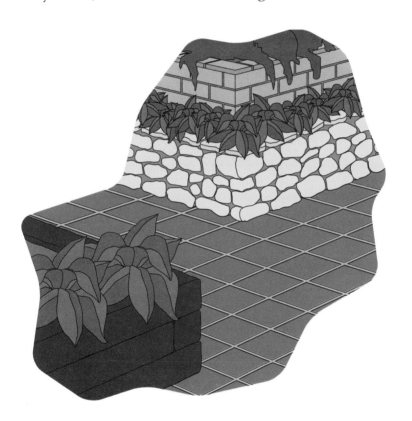

Build with lumber . . .

For a retaining wall, excavate enough soil to allow room to work—about 16 inches from the back of the wall. String a line to mark the outer edge of the wall. Dig postholes every 4 feet or so and at least 2 feet deep (consult local codes). Dig trenches for "deadmen"—the beams that lock into the hillside. Add a shovelful of gravel to each hole, put in the 4×4 or 6×6 posts (leave them long—they'll be trimmed to height later), and fill the holes with concrete, plumbing the posts in both directions. Allow 24 hours for the concrete to set.

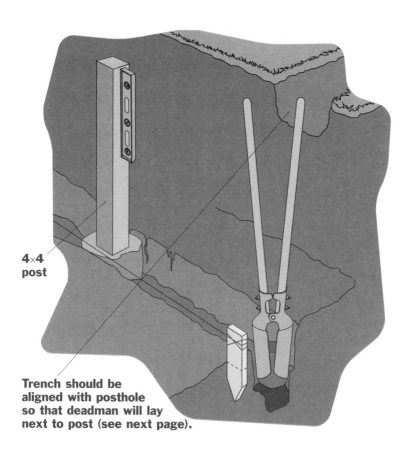

4×4 post

Trench should be aligned with posthole so that deadman will lay next to post (see next page).

For the retaining boards, use pressure-treated lumber or the heartwood of redwood or cedar. Install the deadmen, attaching them to the posts with two ½-inch by 8-inch lag screws. Use a chalk line to mark for uniform height, and trim the posts. Install 2×6 or 2×8 crosspieces and cap the top with a 2×6. Tack filter cloth, felt paper, or building paper to the back of the wall. Place perforated drainage pipe on top of a 2-inch layer of rock to disperse water pressure. Backfill the wall with drain rock or gravel covered with 15-pound building paper or filter cloth.

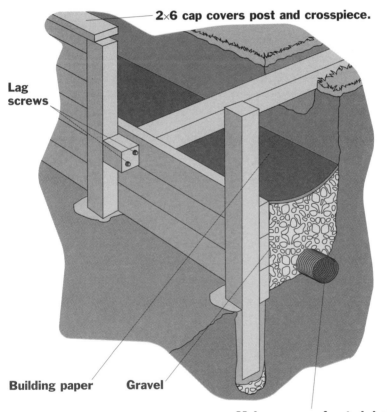

2×6 cap covers post and crosspiece.

Lag screws

Building paper   Gravel

Make sure perforated drain-pipe is pitched to disperse water away from wall.

... or build with timbers

Timbers are easy to work with and are suitable for retaining walls or planters. Use salvaged railroad ties or pressure-treated landscaping timbers specified for ground contact. For a retaining wall, excavate enough soil so that you have ample working space. Next dig trenches for deadmen so they will rest on top of timbers in the upper third of the wall. Then, for either type of wall, string a line and dig a shallow trench so the first timber will sit below final grade. Cover the bottom of the trench with 2 to 4 inches of gravel or crushed drain rock.

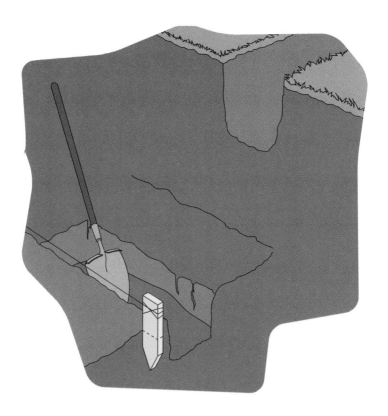

Level the first course of timbers on the gravel. Make a template for drilling 1-inch holes every 3 feet. Mark timbers so the holes will line up, staggering joints by at least 3 feet. Stack the timbers, check that the holes line up, and toenail them on the upslope side with 16-penny (16d) HDG nails. Attach deadmen with countersunk lag bolts. Halfway up, pound lengths of ½-inch galvanized pipe 4 feet into the ground, the tops just below the finished height of the wall. Predrill final timbers and thread them over the pipe.

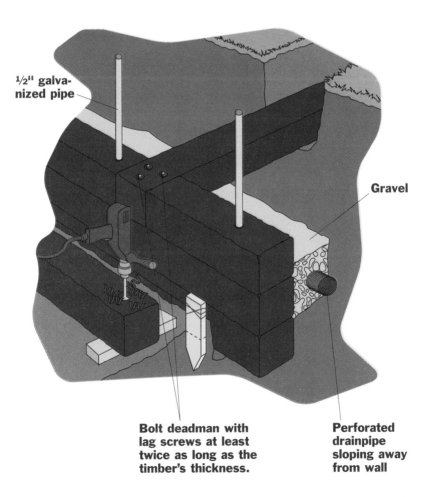

½" galvanized pipe

Gravel

Bolt deadman with lag screws at least twice as long as the timber's thickness.

Perforated drainpipe sloping away from wall

4

. . . or stack stone

Dry-stacked stone walls can be used where the slope is less than 45 degrees and there is little danger of erosion or slippage. The idea is simple: Stack uncut stones so they lean into the slope, and fill in the cracks with soil. Building the wall requires lifting and relifting heavy stones to fit them together, however, which is a time-consuming backbreaker. A variation on this type of wall is to use formed-concrete blocks, which are easier to stack than stone and which interlock for greater stability.

Another type of mortarless stone wall takes a good deal more planning and work. The wall should be "battered"— sloped back toward the top—at a ratio of 2 to 3 inches for every foot of wall height. Dig a trench about 16 inches deep, put in a perforated drainage pipe sloping away from the wall, and cover it with 10 inches of gravel. Use the largest stones for the bottom course; lean subsequent courses downward into the slope. Install filter fabric against the stones, backfill with soil, and place a second drainage pipe about halfway up.

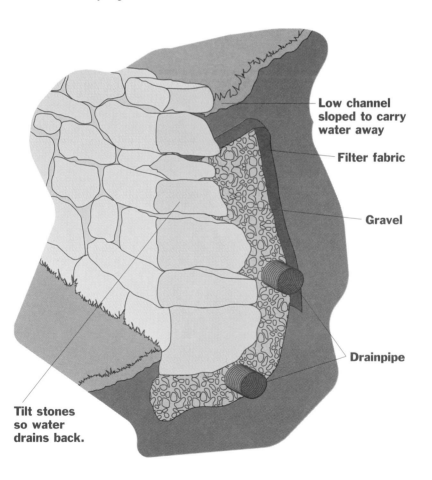

Low channel sloped to carry water away

Filter fabric

Gravel

Drainpipe

Tilt stones so water drains back.

Troubleshooting

Troubleshooting for brick, tile, pavers, & stone

Problem	Solution
Efflorescence (a white, powdery deposit caused when water dissolves the minerals in bricks or pavers and brings them to the surface)	It will disappear in time, but can be eliminated by dry-scrubbing it then hosing it down.
Dried mortar stains	Scrub with a weak solution of muriatic acid and water. Test on a small area first to make sure it doesn't discolor the patio.
Oil and grease stains	Use a garage-floor cleaner (available at an auto parts store).
Cracked tiles, pavers, or bricks	Break out the entire piece with a hammer and cold chisel. If the replacement piece fits too snugly, cut it to allow for expansion.
Cracked mortar joints	Remove the cracked mortar, or "key" it by chiseling out a groove that is wider at the bottom than at the top. Fill with latex-based mortar (a patching compound available at a hardware store).

Troubleshooting for concrete

Problem	Solution
Surface scaling or crazing (the surface of the concrete either flakes away or develops a maze of thin cracks)	Scrape away any loose material. Paint the spot with a latex concrete-bonding agent and allow to dry. Then apply a latex-based mortar with a flat steel trowel.
Cracked concrete	Chisel out any loose material and key the hole. Then apply either a latex-based patching compound, or a mix of 1 part portland cement and 3 parts concrete sand mix.
Drab, uninteresting surface	Paint with concrete paint, adding a contrasting border for interest. Or use the concrete slab as a base for mortaring stone, tile, or brick in place. A low wall bordering the patio, a raised flower bed, planter boxes or pots, or a peninsular planting area cut into the concrete can all add interest to a bleak surface.
Rotted divider boards	Remove rotted dividers with a pry bar and wood chisel, being careful not to mar the concrete. Use a hacksaw or cold chisel to remove any nails embedded in the cavity. Thoroughly sweep and vacuum the cavity before cutting and installing heartwood redwood or cedar replacement dividers, adhering them with spots of construction adhesive every 2 feet.

U.S./Metric Measure Conversions

Formulas for Exact Measures

	Symbol	When you know:	Multiply by:	To find:		Rounded Measures for Quick Reference	
Mass (Weight)	oz	ounces	28.35	grams	1 oz		= 30 g
	lb	pounds	0.45	kilograms	4 oz		= 115 g
	g	grams	0.035	ounces	8 oz		= 225 g
	kg	kilograms	2.2	pounds	16 oz	= 1 lb	= 450 g
					32 oz	= 2 lb	= 900 g
					36 oz	= 2 1/4 lb	= 1000 g (1 kg)
Volume	pt	pints	0.47	liters	1 c	= 8 oz	= 250 ml
	qt	quarts	0.95	liters	2 c (1 pt)	= 16 oz	= 500 ml
	gal	gallons	3.785	liters	4 c (1 qt)	= 32 oz	= 1 liter
	ml	milliliters	0.034	fluid ounces	4 qt (1 gal)	= 128 oz	= 3 3/4 liter
Length	in.	inches	2.54	centimeters	3/8 in.		= 1.0 cm
	ft	feet	30.48	centimeters	1 in.		= 2.5 cm
	yd	yards	0.9144	meters	2 in.		= 5.0 cm
	mi	miles	1.609	kilometers	2 1/2 in.		= 6.5 cm
	km	kilometers	0.621	miles	12 in. (1 ft)		= 30.0 cm
	m	meters	1.094	yards	1 yd		= 90.0 cm
	cm	centimeters	0.39	inches	100 ft		= 30.0 m
					1 mi		= 1.6 km
Temperature	° F	Fahrenheit	5/9 (after subtracting 32)	Celsius	32° F		= 0° C
	° C	Celsius	9/5 (then add 32)	Fahrenheit	212° F		= 100° C
Area	in.²	square inches	6.452	square centimeters	1 in.²		= 6.5 cm²
	ft²	square feet	929.0	square centimeters	1 ft²		= 930 cm²
	yd²	square yards	8361.0	square centimeters	1 yd²		= 8360 cm²
	a.	acres	0.4047	hectares	1 a.		= 4050 m²